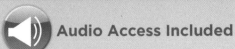
Audio Access Included

# POP FAVORITES
## FOR TENOR SAX

CONTENTS

To access audio visit:
**www.halleonard.com/mylibrary**

Enter Code
7745-7786-0024-9249

Audio Arrangements by Peter Deneff
Tracking, mixing, and mastering by BeatHouse Music

ISBN 978-1-4950-9266-4

7777 W. BLUEMOUND RD. P.O. BOX 13819 MILWAUKEE, WI 53213

Visit Hal Leonard Online at
**www.halleonard.com**

# ACHY BREAKY HEART
## (Don't Tell My Heart)

Words and Music by
DON VON TRESS

# I'M A BELIEVER

Words and Music by
NEIL DIAMOND

**Moderately**

# LA BAMBA

By RITCHIE VALENS

# LOUIE, LOUIE

Words and Music by
RICHARD BERRY

# IMAGINE

Words and Music by
JOHN LENNON

# JAILHOUSE ROCK

Words and Music by JERRY LEIBER
and MIKE STOLLER

# OB-LA-DI, OB-LA-DA

Words and Music by JOHN LENNON
and PAUL McCARTNEY

# SPLISH SPLASH

Words and Music by BOBBY DARIN
and MURRAY KAUFMAN

# STAND BY ME

Words and Music by JERRY LEIBER,
MIKE STOLLER and BEN E. KING

# YELLOW SUBMARINE

Words and Music by JOHN LENNON
and PAUL McCARTNEY

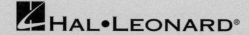

## HAL•LEONARD INSTRUMENTAL PLAY-ALONG

Your favorite songs are arranged just for solo instrumentalists with this outstanding series. Each book includes a great full-accompaniment play-along audio so you can sound just like a pro! Check out **www.halleonard.com** to see all the titles available.

## The Beatles

All You Need Is Love • Blackbird • Day Tripper • Eleanor Rigby • Get Back • Here, There and Everywhere • Hey Jude • I Will • Let It Be • Lucy in the Sky with Diamonds • Ob-La-Di, Ob-La-Da • Penny Lane • Something • Ticket to Ride • Yesterday.

| | | |
|---|---|---|
| _____ 00225330 | Flute . . . . . . . . . . . . . . . | $14.99 |
| _____ 00225331 | Clarinet . . . . . . . . . . . . . | $14.99 |
| _____ 00225332 | Alto Sax . . . . . . . . . . . . . | $14.99 |
| _____ 00225333 | Tenor Sax . . . . . . . . . . . . | $14.99 |
| _____ 00225334 | Trumpet. . . . . . . . . . . . . | $14.99 |
| _____ 00225335 | Horn . . . . . . . . . . . . . . . | $14.99 |
| _____ 00225336 | Trombone . . . . . . . . . . . | $14.99 |
| _____ 00225337 | Violin. . . . . . . . . . . . . . . | $14.99 |
| _____ 00225338 | Viola . . . . . . . . . . . . . . . | $14.99 |
| _____ 00225339 | Cello . . . . . . . . . . . . . . . | $14.99 |

## Chart Hits

All About That Bass • All of Me • Happy • Radioactive • Roar • Say Something • Shake It Off • A Sky Full of Stars • Someone like You • Stay with Me • Thinking Out Loud • Uptown Funk.

| | | |
|---|---|---|
| _____ 00146207 | Flute . . . . . . . . . . . . . . . | $12.99 |
| _____ 00146208 | Clarinet . . . . . . . . . . . . . | $12.99 |
| _____ 00146209 | Alto Sax . . . . . . . . . . . . . | $12.99 |
| _____ 00146210 | Tenor Sax . . . . . . . . . . . . | $12.99 |
| _____ 00146211 | Trumpet. . . . . . . . . . . . . | $12.99 |
| _____ 00146212 | Horn . . . . . . . . . . . . . . . | $12.99 |
| _____ 00146213 | Trombone . . . . . . . . . . . | $12.99 |
| _____ 00146214 | Violin. . . . . . . . . . . . . . . | $12.99 |
| _____ 00146215 | Viola . . . . . . . . . . . . . . . | $12.99 |
| _____ 00146216 | Cello . . . . . . . . . . . . . . . | $12.99 |

## Coldplay

Clocks • Every Teardrop Is a Waterfall • Fix You • In My Place • Lost! • Paradise • The Scientist • Speed of Sound • Trouble • Violet Hill • Viva La Vida • Yellow.

| | | |
|---|---|---|
| _____ 00103337 | Flute . . . . . . . . . . . . . . . | $12.99 |
| _____ 00103338 | Clarinet . . . . . . . . . . . . . | $12.99 |
| _____ 00103339 | Alto Sax . . . . . . . . . . . . . | $12.99 |
| _____ 00103340 | Tenor Sax . . . . . . . . . . . . | $12.99 |
| _____ 00103341 | Trumpet. . . . . . . . . . . . . | $12.99 |
| _____ 00103342 | Horn . . . . . . . . . . . . . . . | $12.99 |
| _____ 00103343 | Trombone . . . . . . . . . . . | $12.99 |
| _____ 00103344 | Violin. . . . . . . . . . . . . . . | $12.99 |
| _____ 00103345 | Viola . . . . . . . . . . . . . . . | $12.99 |
| _____ 00103346 | Cello . . . . . . . . . . . . . . . | $12.99 |

Prices, contents, and availability subject to change without notice.
Disney characters and artwork © Disney Enterprises, Inc.

## Disney Greats

Arabian Nights • Hawaiian Roller Coaster Ride • It's a Small World • Look Through My Eyes • Yo Ho (A Pirate's Life for Me) • and more.

| | | |
|---|---|---|
| _____ 00841934 | Flute . . . . . . . . . . . . . . . | $12.99 |
| _____ 00841935 | Clarinet . . . . . . . . . . . . . | $12.99 |
| _____ 00841936 | Alto Sax . . . . . . . . . . . . . | $12.99 |
| _____ 00841937 | Tenor Sax . . . . . . . . . . . . | $12.95 |
| _____ 00841938 | Trumpet. . . . . . . . . . . . . | $12.99 |
| _____ 00841939 | Horn . . . . . . . . . . . . . . . | $12.99 |
| _____ 00841940 | Trombone . . . . . . . . . . . | $12.95 |
| _____ 00841941 | Violin. . . . . . . . . . . . . . . | $12.99 |
| _____ 00841942 | Viola . . . . . . . . . . . . . . . | $12.99 |
| _____ 00841943 | Cello . . . . . . . . . . . . . . . | $12.99 |
| _____ 00842078 | Oboe . . . . . . . . . . . . . . . | $12.99 |

## Great Themes

Bella's Lullaby • Chariots of Fire • Get Smart • Hawaii Five-O Theme • I Love Lucy • The Odd Couple • Spanish Flea • and more.

| | | |
|---|---|---|
| _____ 00842468 | Flute . . . . . . . . . . . . . . . | $12.99 |
| _____ 00842469 | Clarinet . . . . . . . . . . . . . | $12.99 |
| _____ 00842470 | Alto Sax . . . . . . . . . . . . . | $12.99 |
| _____ 00842471 | Tenor Sax . . . . . . . . . . . . | $12.99 |
| _____ 00842472 | Trumpet. . . . . . . . . . . . . | $12.99 |
| _____ 00842473 | Horn . . . . . . . . . . . . . . . | $12.99 |
| _____ 00842474 | Trombone . . . . . . . . . . . | $12.99 |
| _____ 00842475 | Violin. . . . . . . . . . . . . . . | $12.99 |
| _____ 00842476 | Viola . . . . . . . . . . . . . . . | $12.99 |
| _____ 00842477 | Cello . . . . . . . . . . . . . . . | $12.99 |

## Popular Hits

Breakeven • Fireflies • Halo • Hey, Soul Sister • I Gotta Feeling • I'm Yours • Need You Now • Poker Face • Viva La Vida • You Belong with Me • and more.

| | | |
|---|---|---|
| _____ 00842511 | Flute . . . . . . . . . . . . . . . | $12.99 |
| _____ 00842512 | Clarinet . . . . . . . . . . . . . | $12.99 |
| _____ 00842513 | Alto Sax . . . . . . . . . . . . . | $12.99 |
| _____ 00842514 | Tenor Sax . . . . . . . . . . . . | $12.99 |
| _____ 00842515 | Trumpet. . . . . . . . . . . . . | $12.99 |
| _____ 00842516 | Horn . . . . . . . . . . . . . . . | $12.99 |
| _____ 00842517 | Trombone . . . . . . . . . . . | $12.99 |
| _____ 00842518 | Violin. . . . . . . . . . . . . . . | $12.99 |
| _____ 00842519 | Viola . . . . . . . . . . . . . . . | $12.99 |
| _____ 00842520 | Cello . . . . . . . . . . . . . . . | $12.99 |

## Songs from Frozen, Tangled and Enchanted

Do You Want to Build a Snowman? • For the First Time in Forever • Happy Working Song • I See the Light • In Summer • Let It Go • Mother Knows Best • That's How You Know • True Love's First Kiss • When Will My Life Begin • and more.

| | | |
|---|---|---|
| _____ 00126921 | Flute . . . . . . . . . . . . . . . | $14.99 |
| _____ 00126922 | Clarinet . . . . . . . . . . . . . | $14.99 |
| _____ 00126923 | Alto Sax . . . . . . . . . . . . . | $14.99 |
| _____ 00126924 | Tenor Sax . . . . . . . . . . . . | $14.99 |
| _____ 00126925 | Trumpet. . . . . . . . . . . . . | $14.99 |
| _____ 00126926 | Horn . . . . . . . . . . . . . . . | $14.99 |
| _____ 00126927 | Trombone . . . . . . . . . . . | $14.99 |
| _____ 00126928 | Violin. . . . . . . . . . . . . . . | $14.99 |
| _____ 00126929 | Viola . . . . . . . . . . . . . . . | $14.99 |
| _____ 00126930 | Cello . . . . . . . . . . . . . . . | $14.99 |

## Top Hits

Adventure of a Lifetime • Budapest • Die a Happy Man • Ex's & Oh's • Fight Song • Hello • Let It Go • Love Yourself • One Call Away • Pillowtalk • Stitches • Writing's on the Wall.

| | | |
|---|---|---|
| _____ 00171073 | Flute . . . . . . . . . . . . . . . | $12.99 |
| _____ 00171074 | Clarinet . . . . . . . . . . . . . | $12.99 |
| _____ 00171075 | Alto Sax . . . . . . . . . . . . . | $12.99 |
| _____ 00171106 | Tenor Sax . . . . . . . . . . . . | $12.99 |
| _____ 00171107 | Trumpet. . . . . . . . . . . . . | $12.99 |
| _____ 00171108 | Horn . . . . . . . . . . . . . . . | $12.99 |
| _____ 00171109 | Trombone . . . . . . . . . . . | $12.99 |
| _____ 00171110 | Violin. . . . . . . . . . . . . . . | $12.99 |
| _____ 00171111 | Viola . . . . . . . . . . . . . . . | $12.99 |
| _____ 00171112 | Cello . . . . . . . . . . . . . . . | $12.99 |

## Wicked

As Long As You're Mine • Dancing Through Life • Defying Gravity • For Good • I'm Not That Girl • Popular • The Wizard and I • and more.

| | | |
|---|---|---|
| _____ 00842236 | Flute . . . . . . . . . . . . . . . | $12.99 |
| _____ 00842237 | Clarinet . . . . . . . . . . . . . | $12.99 |
| _____ 00842238 | Alto Saxophone . . . . . . . . | $11.95 |
| _____ 00842239 | Tenor Saxophone. . . . . . . . | $11.95 |
| _____ 00842240 | Trumpet. . . . . . . . . . . . . | $11.99 |
| _____ 00842241 | Horn . . . . . . . . . . . . . . . | $11.95 |
| _____ 00842242 | Trombone . . . . . . . . . . . | $12.99 |
| _____ 00842243 | Violin. . . . . . . . . . . . . . . | $11.99 |
| _____ 00842244 | Viola . . . . . . . . . . . . . . . | $12.99 |
| _____ 00842245 | Cello . . . . . . . . . . . . . . . | $12.99 |

HAL•LEONARD®

0617

# 101 SONGS

## YOUR FAVORITE SONGS ARE ARRANGED FOR SOLO INSTRUMENTALISTS WITH THIS GREAT SERIES.

### 101 BROADWAY SONGS

Cabaret • Do You Hear the People Sing? • Edelweiss • Guys and Dolls • Hello, Dolly! • I Dreamed a Dream • If I Were a Bell • Luck Be a Lady • Ol' Man River • Seasons of Love • Send in the Clowns • Think of Me • Tomorrow • What I Did for Love • and many more.

| | | |
|---|---|---|
| 00154199 | Flute | $14.99 |
| 00154200 | Clarinet | $14.99 |
| 00154201 | Alto Sax | $14.99 |
| 00154202 | Tenor Sax | $14.99 |
| 00154203 | Trumpet | $14.99 |
| 00154204 | Horn | $14.99 |
| 00154205 | Trombone | $14.99 |
| 00154206 | Violin | $14.99 |
| 00154207 | Viola | $14.99 |
| 00154208 | Cello | $14.99 |

### 101 HIT SONGS

All About That Bass • All of Me • Brave • Breakaway • Clocks • Fields of Gold • Firework • Hey, Soul Sister • Ho Hey • I Gotta Feeling • Jar of Hearts • Love Story • 100 Years • Roar • Rolling in the Deep • Shake It Off • Smells like Teen Spirit • Uptown Funk • and more.

| | | |
|---|---|---|
| 00194561 | Flute | $16.99 |
| 00197182 | Clarinet | $16.99 |
| 00197183 | Alto Sax | $16.99 |
| 00197184 | Tenor Sax | $16.99 |
| 00197185 | Trumpet | $16.99 |
| 00197186 | Horn | $16.99 |
| 00197187 | Trombone | $16.99 |
| 00197188 | Violin | $16.99 |
| 00197189 | Viola | $16.99 |
| 00197190 | Cello | $16.99 |

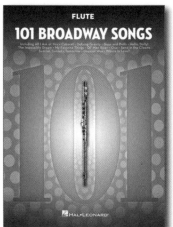

### 101 CLASSICAL THEMES

Ave Maria • Bist du bei mir (You Are with Me) • Canon in D • Clair de Lune • Dance of the Sugar Plum Fairy • 1812 Overture • Eine Kleine Nachtmusik ("Serenade"), First Movement Excerpt • The Flight of the Bumble Bee • Funeral March of a Marionette • Fur Elise • Gymnopedie No. 1 • Jesu, Joy of Man's Desiring • Lullaby • Minuet in G • Ode to Joy • Piano Sonata in C • Pie Jesu • Rondeau • Theme from Swan Lake • Wedding March • William Tell Overture • and many more.

| | | |
|---|---|---|
| 00155315 | Flute | $14.99 |
| 00155317 | Clarinet | $14.99 |
| 00155318 | Alto Sax | $14.99 |
| 00155319 | Tenor Sax | $14.99 |
| 00155320 | Trumpet | $14.99 |
| 00155321 | Horn | $14.99 |
| 00155322 | Trombone | $14.99 |
| 00155323 | Violin | $14.99 |
| 00155324 | Viola | $14.99 |
| 00155325 | Cello | $14.99 |

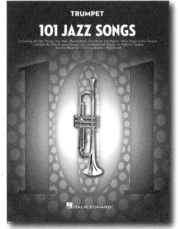

### 101 JAZZ SONGS

All of Me • Autumn Leaves • Bewitched • Blue Skies • Body and Soul • Cheek to Cheek • Come Rain or Come Shine • Don't Get Around Much Anymore • A Fine Romance • Here's to Life • I Could Write a Book • It Could Happen to You • The Lady Is a Tramp • Like Someone in Love • Lullaby of Birdland • The Nearness of You • On Green Dolphin Street • Satin Doll • Stella by Starlight • Tangerine • Unforgettable • The Way You Look Tonight • Yesterdays • and many more.

| | | |
|---|---|---|
| 00146363 | Flute | $14.99 |
| 00146364 | Clarinet | $14.99 |
| 00146366 | Alto Sax | $14.99 |
| 00146367 | Tenor Sax | $14.99 |
| 00146368 | Trumpet | $14.99 |
| 00146369 | Horn | $14.99 |
| 00146370 | Trombone | $14.99 |
| 00146371 | Violin | $14.99 |
| 00146372 | Viola | $14.99 |
| 00146373 | Cello | $14.99 |

**HAL•LEONARD®**

www.halleonard.com

*Prices, contents and availability subject to change without notice.*

O217